REFLECTIONS AND POEMS OF FAITH

Shadeera O. Allen

Shadeera O. Allen
Fort Lauderdale, Florida

Cover Design: Okomota
Editing and Layout: The Self-Publishing Maven
Formatting: István Szabó, Ifj.

ISBN 13: 978-0-692-12746-9
ISBN 10: 0-692-12746-1

Printed in the United States

ACKNOWLEDGEMENTS

In the four corners of this book "Reflections and Poems of Faith," it helped to exercise my spiritual walk with Christ and the benediction of his salvation. As remembrance that the center remains with; God's grace, guidance and the comfort of joy and acknowledging those that have placed a spark in my light through my journey.

This journey I am walking has been a great success and a spiritual phase which carried me to see my faith elevate and the anointing that covered me by the love of God. In the abundance of my praise report, I would like to thank Gloria Wallace for being a true woman of God, mentor, and her dedication she pursues in helping others. Sometimes we never know the strategy of God's plan but He sure does a wonderful job and that was appointing her in my life to keep me focus in the angle of God's kingdom.

Sincere thanks to my bother in Christ Gabriel Jackson, for his sufficient prayers, reassurance I stayed at the foot of Jesus.

In advance, "The Self Publishing Maven", call to commitment, well-driven and the ability to helping others toward a person life transition for writing. I thank you for encouraging me in my writing; as it shows because it brought the best out of me and my writing skills. Most of all, my mother Ophelia Allen for being genuinely positive and active about the aspect of my life which enhanced me to be where I am on today.

DEDICATION

To my beloved daughters Ja'Ziah and Ominique, my love for you both is endless. May God and His angels continue to watch over you both as you grow together as sisters and young ladies who walk in God's glory.

INTRODUCTION

Life can bring changes in the supplement of good and bad but the affirmation of changes will justify itself by the "definition to reality." What do I mean that affirmation of changes will justify itself by its "definition to reality?" Look at it this way, when life throws a stone in the view of your faith you have the advantage to cast a stone back or believe the process going to be successful and helping to strengthen you! So...I do believe that the affirmation is a "definition to reality" in my life and yours too because we have the choice to improve and declare the things we're striving for in these trying times.

Your life is no longer labeled as a woman wearing a veil to the secrets or regrets that are haunting you, or a man being intimidated by the gesture of their choices. We are not perfect. As it speaks:

1 Thessalonians 5:11, "Therefore, encourage one another and build each other up, just as in fact you are doing."

Be of courage everyone. Let us be the world volume to fill the gaps of Faith, the radius of our reflections and the equation to the affirmations of our destiny.

Contents

FAITH

ANOTHER STORM

The rain continued to fall,
The trees embrace the direction of the wind,
The ground still remained the same but what changed were the clouds and the movement of its gravity.

Honestly, I enjoy the rain when it comes because it's like a change appears as to the end of the road that continues to grow.

Thinking positive: "What do you see at the end of your road?" Does it continue or stop? If it continues, what are your pros or cons? If it stops, what are some things you would change and why? Think about it.

"Am I, Pronounced To Be Given or Taken?"

It's unfortunate to say when a man doesn't want to love in particular. Why, wait?

It's obviously strange when they try to negotiate or figure you out by assuming if you are or not the one for them. Rather than leaving it in God's hands and allowing Him to do until his will but only given on his time and not your own.

On this occasion I am "taken" and that's by God and not by man. Don't let go of God's unchanging hands because we can be quite impatient but weary at the same time. It's like feeling complete and discerning our Boaz is being positioned in the right place at its right timing There's time you have felt blue but with all necessary we ought to be satisfied and accepted to being single and walking into the path of glory.

RELATIONSHIP WITH A WOMAN OR A MAN

Love never fails when it's there but the feelings remain if it's real.

Encourage the soul.

Embrace your heart.

Allow God to wrap His arms around with care and your relationship as well.

Give it time to grow through the process in order for things to work according to Him.

Push forth towards positive surroundings.

Continue to be humble about being in the process to visualize the work of putting your effort into it and not compromising.

Together your purpose ought to be a way to loving one another unconditional and the passion to giving your all to Christ for him to make your relationship in a sufficient but delicate way.

That's doing it the right way; I was well impressed about this scripture verse Colossians 3:23-24: And whatsoever ye do, do it heartily, as to the Lord, and not unto men; Knowing that of the Lord ye shall receive the reward of the inheritance: for ye serve the Lord Christ.

Trusting that He is already doing it for you, big blessing to come in the way, like David dance!

HERON BIRD

Against the wind his wings stretched out high as an eagle.

There he goes bold, ambitious and sturdy.
Where his feathers were driven by my eyes and I recall his feathers were as white as snow but fluffed as cotton.

Against the wind there he goes...among the life of its desire.
The siren of the ambulance.
The outrageous traffic.
The switching of the lights.
The gas that we're inhaling.
The motor from the car which trembles the thoughts.

He's not afraid.
He's not alone.
He has a purpose.
He has a message.
For he's not alone.

But several things I noticed about this bird...

When I sing, his gesture changed as his neck reached for the melody of my voice.
When I gave a tune his attention aroused more towards the pitch.

But once the bird heard the ignition change it began to fly against the wind!

WHO I AM

-Trust and Obey-

Who am I to say, you are defiled.
Who am I to say, you have failed his command.
Who am I?

Who am I to justify?
Who am I to blame which by the hands of filth but are now cleansed?
Who am I to point fingers at someone else rather than pointing them to myself?

Be delight. Be uplifted. Be righteous. Be fully committed.

For the Lord has taken me on and through the journeys' and still continuing.

He will do the same for you!

He is Able; He is real"

THE BLOWING WIND

Inhaling (grace) fulfilled within Nature,
Proclaim its' presence of shallow loops,
Grasps, of the wind swiftness that is of a great Blow,
I am holding on to you.

Listening to the flow of its vocal
Began to express the wave's gravity that starts from a note?
Words can't reconcile of how I feel,
Potential faith, is the reality of life,
You're an ostinato.

The wind elevated
The sky turned "Purple".

This is a change.

A SOARING EAGLE

If we could just trust in God on the vision He put forth then we shouldn't be dismay or focused about the situation it causes. It comes to being content as pursuing the things He has positioned in your life.

I am a witness.

Making steps to becoming successful through the spirit of faith which inspires you to being ambitious about your future. Yes, a part of your journey can sometimes be with disappointments but it only helps you to maintain the "definition of reality" and the ability to being stronger. This can benefit to include the principal of "A Soaring Eagle" to taking you at the next level. So as I experienced but gone through it, I soared as an eagle because I've made it and gave all my might to set forth at the mark! You can do it, too but you must believe and soar.

GOD MADE HEAVEN AND EARTH

Great gesture to know that he is "Able" and "Possible" to see all his magnificent creations of divine seed that grows here on earth because when you teach it, you can see how developed it has grown and to know why it's still standing. What causes the greatness of God and his loving, tender, grace and mercy he shows.

SPIRITUAL WAYS

Day by day it took a lot of energy from me because I was holding back the tears and the pain I held in. Not saying, that I wasn't grateful or happy but I would love to have a loving person in my life to understand the things I'm going through. Oh boy was it challenging my faith, but I made it through.

BENEATH THE SUN AND BELOW THE MOON

Even though, the things we pray for isn't the promise He's directing us to but living in this world on today, we must keep ourselves in check with the desire to the things God call upon our lives because it's changing. Some changes are good but otherwise we should be the light of the world and not the darkness neither the enemy of each of other. Let's have more of a brotherly love than hatred and sisterly blessing than jealously so we all are as one and collectively become the light of the moon.

"Be the shine of all things that we set among and the light at the end of the moon".

DESTINED FOR COMPLETE VICTORY...

Sometimes we may have felt that we failed at the angle of the road to success. You have to get back up to face your setback, fight your combat and overcome in complete victory! Don't forget our everyday guidance; that's the Lord will. He will never leave you in such way you can't see yourself out of a situation because he will always lean a hand.

I believe that the road we choose isn't always the way to go but we have the ability to pray and ask for clarity and the vision of going the right direction. The right way, the way of creating a stand point in your life to sustaining growth in being successful to overcoming trials that we all go through to making a change. The question to knowing when we're in complete victory, how would we retain the quality of being victoriously successful in the process.

ADMITTING

In the clouds of joy, I reach so high
The glory and power comes from the Lord.
Lord, I am asking you on tonight to forgive me for my sins
that I have made, said or done. But Lord for this man that is
in my life at this moment, give me his understanding. Lord
please shows me if he is the husband you grant in my life or
is it just something I would need to leave to destiny?

For, I shall get on my knees tonight before bed and pray for
him as he should pray for me that I forgive him and he for-
gives me; forgiving us for our sins and confusion because we
know that you aren't a God of confusion.

And Lord…my love for him is overwhelming but will he ac-
cept that…or will he just walk away. Lord, if you grant Mr.
Henry to be a part of my life and to be a father to my child it
is only in your Will. So I leave my diary tonight with a smile
because God you have done miracles and healed me com-
pletely. I smile.
My questions wait.

My answer shows itself and no he is not the one God has
chosen for me.

I WAS TOLD BY A MAN...

Wisdom.

As the conversation begins it was not intentionally to make an assignment but to hear the words of wisdom that God placed in my heart to give to [him]. Not knowing of this man by any of his circumstances, problems or lifestyle but what I have learned that God reigns on the just and the unjust.

I just thank him for his mercy and the light he has brought to know that he is God.

CARNATION FLOWERS

Desperately, I needed a loan.

This irritated me so much but I remember God saying, "He wouldn't put any more on us than we can bear" breathing calmly with a rational outcome.

As I have experienced with men they speculate you must have a lot going on which we should have a positive view of ourselves and the future. But come on…at the same time you must too! Being a woman you're doing the best you can as a parent, single mother and a role model to someone.

Genuinely,
I started to sing to myself, "I have some good days…I have some hills to climb…I have some bad days …I won't complain". I thank God for the melody He placed in my heart to help press my way through. Smiles. Approaching work there they were my "carnation flowers", released the pain. No anxiety.

God does all things!

Guess what? He blessed me with extra earnings and endurance to understand how to lean on biblical faith and trusting in Him only.

THE DEPTH OF THE VALLEY

Holding on to what we know best and learning the process; fruits of the spirit to help sustain our walk to lasting the appearance for the calling of our purpose. In life we live this fantasy; going to be possible in making or a command. As usual by the time you try to figure it out, it began to fall apart and become a leash. Why, I say because you must realize that everything you have in the power to do doesn't always come through but with God put first it's possible. When reality begins, you will see a change in yourself by trusting, believing and having faith in Him either in good times or bad times. I am continuing to learn the process of fruits of the spirit led by God.

"Some delusions will become faults, but your faults will turn to be a lesson learned".

BETWEEN THE ENEMY AND THE DEVIL

What an experience I have had of this and the thought of knowing when God is in control you must let him in at all times. Individuals will do their best to consume your vision and the gift God has for you; inspiring, motivating, your character, your belief, your foundation of life.

Oh yes, many other things, too. But you must know the difference between the enemy and the devil itself because sometimes if we don't know any better we gather our main view on thinking too much instead of seeing it right in front of us. What I am stating in such language is that sometimes God does things to put forth to test our faith. Then again the devil makes an issue to become bigger than what it is, because he tries to make someone your enemy to destroy what God has for you. So be careful of your mind frame. He above is Mighty!

The Enemy: Brings forth judgmental situations and tries to dictate your integrity. But feel he/she has won a victory and power which is not by God.

The Devil: A deceiver.

You better be careful whose opening your doors.
Read: Job 2:1-10 KJV

REFLECTIONS

POETRY

A Tea party…

    A Tea party!

What is that? I need to know because there are so much we the women of; winning towards victory on the behalf of our faith need to discuss. Did you ever think women's just compromise the situation but treasure the problem to giving into particular things to make it convenient? We have to be established and ready to conquer the fight through faith and the ability to grow by measure.

    When?
        Where?

Girl, tell me all about it.

Oh… okay a Tea Party is a group of ladies that gather together which come around the table to sit, enjoy a cup of tea, laugh, chat and express their feelings about life.

Wow!

Girl, hush your mouth!

This sounds like fun and a priority to set an example for other ladies like us which this will help being supportive to one another.

So can I come?

Girl I will be there to help benefit the factors of being a successful woman and declare my faith.

Ladies,

Ladies,

Ladies,

Let me tell you something while I am standing right here looking good.

Sophisticated.
Sassy.

A WINNING RACE

Acknowledging the things, I have and the consecration to focus on the visual of his promise. As our patience are being challenged by people and things that are in counterfeit on each and every day of our live and we must stay in the race!

Appreciating the path He has chosen for you, knowing the process of your life and the approach to different scenarios.

Understanding what God is guiding through to accomplish all greater things in life to become successful; established you to being productive in the adversary of our stewardship

It is youto accept the truth rather than a lie.

As God said "Lean not unto your own understanding", which is so.

"My obstacles are blocked but my success is in a clear zone".

Dear Lord,

For the days I've been counting, you were there.
For the months that have been rolling over, you keep me.
For the times you have been in the mist during good and bad times I am still depending on you; you are God.

For the greatness of your power you've given,
For the sickness you have removed as you healed from nation to nation.

You are marvelous.

For the times when finance wasn't at its best you were still there and provided.
For the troubled moments in my life you took away but by faith and mercy from destruction you mold me.

And from darkness to light, "let go and let God have his way".

Amen.
Tears.

Praise Him!

When the devil tries to come into your territory you must tell him "I rebuke you in the name of Jesus!" yet get behind thee and send whatever he is trying to do back to HELL. Let him know that the spirit of the Lord is in this place and that it shall be glory and peace in your presence. Give God that ridiculous praise that crazy praise.

In the name of Jesus! While you start shouting around you just thank Him.
I've been changed.

LADY IN PINK

Let the colors of spring brighten your day,
Because it starts with the words others to say,
For the things that are colorful can demonstrate the beauty
of life.
Soften the heart that helps you to live.
Embrace the arms that hold you so dear.
Love of love that gives so much joy.

By the sweet songs that are mentioned of many words
touched.

Remember this day,
Remember this time,
Remember the individuals that you surround.

We're here to develop growth,
We're here to sustain strength,
We're here to be loved that's why we are so dear.

With that said we're here to acknowledge all of our goals.

Celebrate. Celebrate. Celebrate.

MY DEVOTION

To God is the glory! I get so bubbled inside when I think about him; it's like fire in your bones and you can't stop moving and that's the Holy Spirit in you that just takes over and when it does you get so excited you just can't tell it.

What I am saying to everyone reading this book is that you shouldn't put your life on hold for anyone.

Yes, I have experienced some things already and it's not to break you but to show you what's ahead of you in life and that these things will come upon you so you must be prepared. Don't contemplate a person's feelings or their thought's, but do it for you.

I am not ashamed.
I won't give up.
I will not let go.
I am here for a purpose.
I don't expect things.
I can do all things that strengthen me.
You're gaining.

HEALING PROCESS

No one to depend on,
Understanding life is not easy,
Appreciating the things, He placed in my life, accepting the
facts which brought me a long way.

I am still standing.

He has given me genuine love,
He shows the vision,
He showers His Miracles as He continues to anoint me with
meekness, humbleness and peace.

I am blessed to be healed by the power of God.

And He did!

Entering the Ob/GYN private doctor's office not knowing
the cost but understood it was worth it. Because the God I
serve, He is righteous and above all things. Truly, I didn't
know how I was going to afford it and God turned that
around.

Yes, He did. Have closeness with Him.

Quoting to myself, "Lord you said you will never leave me
nor forsake me". But what He did became a miracle. It began

while the Nurse Practitioner took a few minutes outside of the room; as the Lord spoke to me saying, "My child… why must you worry." For I am God, you are healed. This test was worth it to know. As you trusted me and believed in me.

Oh my child you are healed.
My eyes were flooded with tears as I listened.

And yes, surely when the nurse came into the room she gazed at me with a look as if someone had exchanged results as peace comforted her.

I smiled.

To those that are reading this wait on the Lord and He shall renew your strength as to understanding God never makes mistakes.

"Sweet Potato Pie"

I just want to take the time out and thank God for many things. They are great things to recall and that's being grateful for life itself and the greatness it holds.

Bearing all the violence,
Bearing all the crimes,
Bearing all the situations we are accustom, too.
Knowing he wouldn't put anything on us that we couldn't bear.

That I must mention that I look to God and not to understand the situation He has positioned because he takes us through paths to show you just how great He is and to test our faith. Knowing how to go about it by not choosing our own green pastures but allowing Him above to lead us the way.

SUBJECT: GRATEFUL

Interview of Workplace

Today began the second day that God had spoken to me and not only was it his voice which I heard but it was in his Will he announced to me to accept, adhere and understand because he knew I would do his Will. That I was aware and warning my family of the new changes that were coming next and that this was what God and my grandmother Ethel Strachan wanted.

It's common to say that God speaks to you…
As I approached my work desk God said "Shadeera this day will be a day to remember…This day will be a day of happiness…This day will be a celebration…This day will be your birthday and on that day October 9, 2011 your grandmother will come home to be with me." I paused. My eyes were filled with tears and my mouth dry and as I smiled I spoke back to God and said: "Yes, I accept." Stating in confidence because I understood this was God's Will and not mine.

Tears of Joy you're not alone.

WALKING OVER WATER PHASE I

This was amazing. I sigh. This came about with my cousin Tesha who I have always been close with even though we have our own differences. Needless to say what I saw was real.

Truly, it was troubled water and God needed me to inform Tesha about her situation that she was trying to defeat, but she did not understand that our battles aren't ours to defeat alone, but with the Lord! I experienced for the first time I was walking on water while I kept my eyes on Him. I have seen! There I stand in the middle of the ocean... oh, how extraordinary it was...as God stood in the middle and I was to the left side of him and Tesha was on the right side of him, she was looking sad and weary and on the other side of Tesha was a child. It was in God's Will to perform the duty for me to uplift her and to follow through of what he told me to do.

WALKING OVER WATER PHASE II

As the dream revealed Tesha and I were standing in the mist at a Theme park in Orlando, Florida. In the dream, God was showing the present before the thought of going. Once again, Tesha, the kids and I were planning a trip to one of the theme parks. People were enjoying the attractions, touring of the park and the amazement of the rides but what took forth wasn't good at all. So as I stormed quickly over to Tesha I was trying to tell her about the danger that God told me to inform her about the Park. Thank God we didn't decide to go but still in the dream I pointed out the wires from the pole that were deadly and what I was telling her to not go on one of the rides she was going on, sure enough, she did not take my advice and took it upon herself to go…within those minutes passing all I could see were that the wires were falling down from the pole towards Tesha and I dropped everything and ran over to her from solid ground to troubled water. But while I ran towards the water I was walking and jumping from every other white cushion trying to make it to her and honestly when I finally reached her she was covered with a white blanket over her as well as dressed in all white lying on the stretcher without any movement. Crying out to Tesha, "Wake up, wake up Tesha it's me", and with the communication only me and God could understand I spoke to her the words he told me to say. Testimony Saints! Don't you know when he has given me the words to say, I touched Tesha with my hands and here she woke up.

Remember only God has the power in His hands. I gave God all the glory, honor and praise because I believe and know that God has all Power!

SHOWERING DOWN BLESSING'S

There I lie in the bed of ease that took my thoughts away from ordinary things. I just don't know how much more I can thank Him. My God is AWESOME. You know when you are all choked up over words well in my case I am all choked for Him and giving all the praise. There will be sometimes when you may go through something in order for God to show you how great he is and the things he can do, such as; faith, praying, living/walking in Christ, trust him only, allowing him to come into your life by acceptance.

Let me leave my journal some space for you all, out there so that you have the opportunity to admit to God the things he can do, will do, and are doing.

Be Blessed.

Short Poem: An Impassed Corner

From the four corners that are performed to working purposes hides the beauty of God's Holy temple. It is great to be from those corners because it is set as a blockage but with his grace and mercy he that brought life in us. With the grace and mercy, he has opened doors for marvelous things but closes the doors that are to be shut.

A FAMILY'S RECIPE

May the season be full of greatness and joy!
For the day comes around every year with a bit of spice and laughter.
With the gatherings of Family and Friends,
Grandmother's love of sugar treats sprinkled inside of her bin,
Papa's old greasy socks stashed with a hole in between his toes,
Oh boy!
What laughter. I am tickled.
Smelling the garnish of yummy sweet potato pies,
Inhaling the honey baked glazed ham,
Hearing the babies cry,
Listening to cousins' Clichéd jokes,
Oh boy! Oh boy!
What a Christmas to be jolly.
I remember…
Can we all remember the great times and the new beginning of family time?
Digesting your inheritance,
Intellect the fullness of good Deeds,
Enduring Yankee candles of "Vanilla bean" that melts of sweet drops.

Oh boy! Oh boy! Oh boy! Oh boy! What a Merry Christmas to beginning.
Poetry:

KNEELING TO THE HOLY THRONE

Now you see a lost soul that needs to be found but how crazy to fulfill the devil when he is not our Savior so when we are lost we must encourage the flesh to be saved, steadfast, receive knowledge and pray for a closer walk. That we may accomplish the mission God gave us to do and remembering it is in his Will and his way. I saw the children of God at the altar crying out to Him.

MY HERITAGE

Breath...

The fresh air we all breath together,

When you're feeling pain,

I just know the remedy to take that away,

And

That was grandma love that taught us to say, "Baby, it's going to be alright".

After getting several lessons about how to do right, it was granddad that said: "Boy, you better pull those bridges up and be a man".

I paused.

Because I had to think about just what life meant and how much our grandparents, parents, aunt and uncle were saying to be somebody and make the right choices in life.

Grow.

Making best decisions to enhance your everyday judgement on agendas we take on...

Learn.

Learn by the lessons you quite didn't understand because by grandma and granddad they always had a plan.

They live, they remain strong because as they left behind a legacy to move the family on.

Affirmations

My Vision is Clear

I Pursue Purpose

I Have The Strength
Of A "Butterfly"

God Is My Miracle Worker

I Am Worth It

I Get My Guidance
From God

God Is Leading
The Way

I Am Making
Better Decisions

I Am Forever Loved

I Embrace God's Journey and Promise

I Am Destined To Have A Victorious Year

I Will Reach
My Daily Goals

I am Trustworthy

I am Flying Above

I am Pushing and Striving

I am Chosen One

I have A Great Heart

I Have Purpose

Abundance is Mine

I am Prospering from
My Daily Tasks

I am Walking in
My Purpose

Today! I Accept Change

www.ingramcontent.com/pod-product-compliance
Lightning Source LLC
Chambersburg PA
CBHW061158040426
42445CB00013B/1713